My H Is Dying

PRAYERS AND REFLECTIONS

Mary E. Latela

One Liguori Drive
Liguori, MO 63057-9999
(314) 464-2500

LIGUORI
PUBLICATIONS

For Rose

ISBN 0-89243-517-8
Library of Congress Catalog Card Number: 92-75204

Copyright © 1993, Liguori Publications
Printed in the United States of America

Scripture texts used in this work are taken from GOOD NEWS BIBLE, Today's English Version, copyright © 1976, by the American Bible Society, New York, New York, and are used with permission. All rights reserved.

Cover design by Christine Kraus

Contents

Introduction

My dear reader,

You have learned that a friend is dying. You don't know what to say; you don't know what to think. You are experiencing a kaleidoscope of emotions. One thing you know for certain is that you will not abandon your friend at this time when they need you most.

This booklet is intended for prayer and reflection directed toward the process your friend is experiencing. You can use this booklet when you are alone and the sense of impending loss weighs heavily. You can shed your tears freely; you can pound pillows because the death of your friend seems so unfair. However, your prayers for them are vital; they need your spiritual support more than ever.

In addition, visit and call your friend. Many people avoid contact with even a close friend at such a time because they "don't know what to say." You don't have to know ahead of time what to say; the right words will come. Nor do you need to say much at all. The important thing is to be there, to sit and hold your friend's hand, to exchange a hug, to pray. Stay to the very end—and beyond. You will experience something very special, the privilege of helping your friend make the transition from this earthly life into the fullness of the kingdom heaven.

May our gracious God bless you and keep you strong.

Prayerfully,

Mary E. Latela

Mary E. Latela

[Note: In order to make the prayers and reflections in this booklet suitable for a terminally ill friend of either gender and to facilitate smoother reading, we have chosen to use the pronouns "they," "them," and "their" in the singular sense instead of "he or she," "him or her," and "his or hers."]

God Is With Us Forever

Scripture *Even before the world was made, God had already chosen us to be his through our union with Christ, so that we would be holy and without fault before him.*

(Ephesians 1:4)

Prayer | Lord, be with my friend who is sick. You have chosen them from all eternity. You have called them into being and chosen to love them with a closeness that will never die. They need your closeness now, more than ever. Help them feel your loving hands, the same hands that fashioned them, now leading them, carrying them closer to you.

Psalm | "A Prayer of Humble Trust"
LORD, I have given up my pride
  and turned away from my arrogance.
I am not concerned with great matters
  or with subjects too difficult for me.
Instead, I am content and at peace.
As a child lies quietly in its mother's arms,
  so my heart is quiet within me.
Israel, trust in the LORD
  now and forever!

(Psalm 131)

Reflection | A French song says, "Bless the night when out of two people of flesh you formed us, called us to be yours. Bless the night when you will call us home to be with you forever."

Sometimes we forget that you willed our existence from all eternity, that you selected our parents and lovingly brought

6

them together so that we would have life. Before we ever existed, God knew about us and held our invisible hands, soon to have life in them forever. God is still there, holding our human, hurting hands. The Lord continues to lead us, to carry us home to himself.

Pause awhile and rest in the Lord's presence.

Quiet

Gracious God, assure my friend in their illness. Open the floodgates of your love and convince them that you have chosen them and that you will always be there to lead them to yourself. I ask this humbly in the name of my friend _____ through Jesus Christ, my Lord. Amen.

Closing Prayer

We Have Nothing to Fear

Scripture | *Suddenly a strong wind blew down on the lake, and the boat began to fill with water, so that they were all in great danger. The disciples went to Jesus and woke him up, saying, "Master, Master! We are about to die!" Jesus got up and gave an order to the wind and to the stormy water; they quieted down, and there was a great calm.*

(Luke 8:23-24)

Prayer | Lord, be with my friend who is so afraid. They feel as if they are in the middle of a storm—alone—that perhaps you are asleep. Assure them that you are awake and aware of how they are feeling, that you can fill them with peace, that you can fill them with a great calm.

Psalm | "A Prayer of Praise"
The LORD is my light and my salvation;
  I will fear no one.
The LORD protects me from all danger;
  I will never be afraid.

(from Psalm 27)

Reflection | My friend is afraid. Like many others who are dealing with impending death, they have acknowledged that they have a choice—to fight as hard as they can to the very end or to concede, to lie back and wait to die.

My friend's calendar is filled now with medical appointments and trips to the hospital. Schedules revolve around living and dying. The kitchen counter is covered with vials of medicine instead of the usual implements for meal preparation.

Sometimes we are afraid because we forget that the Lord is always with us, is able to calm our anxiety—no matter how fearful we become. Even while waiting to see the physician, waiting for the test results, waiting to fall asleep when we are too exhausted to sleep, we can be wrapped in the calm the Lord brings to his special friends.

Pause awhile and rest in the Lord's presence.

Quiet

Gracious God, quiet my friend in their fearfulness. Take away the terror of the unknown, calm the storms. Keep them strong when the treatments seem more painful than the illness. Wrap them in peace. I ask this humbly in the name of my friend _____ through Jesus Christ, my Lord. Amen.

Closing Prayer

We Will Live for All Eternity

Scripture | *But if Christ lives in you, the Spirit is life for you because you have been put right with God....*

(Romans 8:10)

Prayer | Lord, in their own way, my friend has indicated that they know they are dying. They know the truth—that they will not live to see another Christmas or another birthday, that they might not live to see the spring rains, the roses of summer, autumn with its pumpkins and scarlet-and-golden leaves. They will not need a calendar for next year because they will no longer be limited by our kind of time—days and months and years.

Psalm | "A Prayer of Confidence"
And so I am thankful and glad,
   and I feel completely secure,
because you protect me
      from the power of death.
I have served you faithfully,
   and you will not abandon me
      to the world of the dead.

You will show me the path
   that leads to life;
   your presence fills me with joy
   and brings me pleasure forever.

(from Psalm 16)

Reflection | It is human and natural to deny the reality of death, to face the fact that our time on earth is coming to an end. We need to remember that the kingdom of God is now and forever.

When our earthly existence is marked by our death, life does not end—eternity takes over. Those who die understand the idea of "eternity" before the rest of us. They will understand experientially what theologians who have spent their lives studying theology are unable to fathom.

Pause and rest awhile in the Lord's presence.

Quiet

Gracious God, help my friend to cling to this life to the very last moment, to squeeze every bit of meaning out of every day on this earth. When they close their eyes for the last time, they will awaken and be welcomed into eternal life. I ask this humbly in the name of my friend _____ through Jesus Christ, my Lord. Amen.

Closing Prayer

God Grants Us Courage

Scripture | *Be alert, stand firm in the faith, be brave, be strong. Do all your work in love.*

(1 Corinthians 16:13-14)

Prayer | Lord, my friend is a courageous person who has had to handle all the ordinary challenges of human beings. But now, Lord, we're talking about my friend's life and death. Give them courage now. They would have given their own life in a moment to save a friend. Now they are fighting for their own life. I ask that you grant them a strong dose of courage NOW when they need so much for you to be there to lift their spirits.

Psalm | "Morning Prayer for Help"
But you, O LORD, are always my
   shield from danger;
  you give me victory
  and restore my courage.
I call to the LORD for help,
  and from his sacred hill he answers me.

(from Psalm 3)

Reflection | It's such a paradox. I beg the Lord to grant my friend the courage to face the final days as they have faced every day, knowing that the final day on earth is coming soon.

All who care deeply about my friend need courage these days in their presence. Not that we should hide our feelings; it's okay to wipe away a tear or to express honest and real anger about a situation that is out of our human hands. The last thing we—or our friend—need is the false bravado before the final act of an opera that ends in tragedy. However, we need the Lord's help to support our friend—in their tears, their sadness, their confusion, their perseverance—thereby giving them the strength to be the person they are.

Pause and rest awhile in the Lord's presence.

Gracious God, I have never witnessed my friend lacking courage, but they must feel that way sometimes. Like most of us, they have their own insecurities. Lord, take away the insecurities—which are real and realistic. Grant them your courage. I ask this humbly in the name of my friend _____ through Jesus Christ, my Lord. Amen.

Quiet

Closing
Prayer

We Are Allowed to Be Angry With God

Scripture | *For I am certain that nothing can separate us from his love: neither death nor life, neither angels nor other heavenly rulers or powers, neither the present nor the future, neither the world above nor the world below—there is nothing in all creation that will ever be able to separate us from the love of God which is ours through Christ Jesus our Lord.*

(Romans 8:38-39)

Prayer | Strengthen my friend. They are usually even-tempered, but they get angry from time to time when their strength wanes and they cannot do some of the simple things that they have always done with ease. Encourage them to share their anger openly with you, knowing that nothing, including that anger, can ever cause you to love them less. Help them to feel sure of your loving acceptance, no matter how they feel, no matter how angry they feel at times.

Psalm | "A Cry of Anguish"
My God, my God, why have you abandoned me?
I have cried desperately for help,
   but still it does not come.
During the day I call to you, my God,
   but you do not answer.
I call at night, but get no rest.

(from Psalm 22)

Sometimes when we are in pain, someone is responsible for our anguish; sometimes we look around for someone to blame.

Reflection

When we are suffering, when we are gravely ill, we may be very angry at God. We need to realize that this time of pain and sorrow is not related at all to how much God loves us. Nothing can diminish or take away that everlasting, unconditional love that caused God to create us.

With the Lord, we can be sure that, because of that great love, we are free to be ourselves—to cry, to complain, even to say, "I've had enough."

Pause and rest awhile in the Lord's presence.

Quiet

Gracious God, assure my friend that they can openly share all feelings with you—even anger and abandonment—and you will not love them less. Were it possible, you would love them even more for their honesty and openness. I ask this humbly in the name of my friend _____ through Jesus Christ, my Lord. Amen.

Closing Prayer

Love Is Our Legacy

Scripture | *Love is patient and kind; it is not jealous or conceited or proud; love is not ill-mannered or selfish or irritable; love does not keep a record of wrongs; love is not happy with evil, but is happy with the truth. Love never gives up; and its faith, hope, and patience never fail.*

(1 Corinthians 13:4-7)

Prayer | Lord, my friend knows all about love—knows what it is and what it is not. Shower them with your love, Lord. Assure them that you really know them and find so much in them to love, just as they have recognized so much to love in others.

Psalm | "God's Complete Knowledge and Care"
LORD, you have examined me and you know me.
You know everything I do;
  from far away you understand
    all my thoughts....
Your knowledge of me is too deep;
  it is beyond my understanding.

(from Psalm 139)

Reflection | When we die, we leave behind a legacy based on how we have lived. We are all imperfect, but our sincere love can outshine our flaws. It could be helpful to realize that when we are dying, our capacity to give and receive love is not impaired. In fact, we may be able to give love even more fully, more purely. Learning to be loving involves gaining the capacity to see life in perspective— what is truly important and what doesn't count at all. What is the point of jealousy or conceit? Why count up the "wrongs" when there are so many more "rights"?

16

Pause and rest awhile in the Lord's presence.

Gracious God, we know that love never gives up. Grant my friend such an abundance of love that they will never be in short supply. At the same time, do not erase all their other feelings—the anger, the depression, the sense of loss—these are appropriate. After they are gone and we are grieving, remind us of the legacy of love they have left behind. I ask this humbly in the name of my friend _____ through Jesus Christ, my Lord. Amen.

Quiet

Closing
Prayer

God Is With Us in Our Sadness

Scripture | *Mary arrived where Jesus was, and as soon as she saw him, she fell at his feet. "Lord," she said, "if you had been here, my brother [Lazarus] would not have died!" Jesus saw her weeping, and he saw how the people with her were weeping also; his heart was touched, and he was deeply moved....Jesus wept. "See how much he loved him!" the people said.*

(John 11:32-36)

Prayer | Lord, be with my friend in their sadness. They are worried about leaving behind the people they love the most dearly—family and friends. Those who survive them will be heartbroken when my friend's heart stops beating. Funeral arrangements will have to be made; the house must be prepared to welcome the people who come out of love to pay their respects. Lord, I do not ask you to cheer up my friend in their state of sadness—that would be artificial. Simply assure the survivors that all the strength they need—and more—to face the days ahead will be given to them.

Psalm | "The Prayer of [One] in Exile"
Why am I so sad?
  Why am I so troubled?
I will put my hope in God,
  and once again I will praise him,
  my savior and my God.

(from Psalm 42)

We all have a right to be sad at the prospect of great loss, the loss of a dear loved one. And the prospect of others grieving over one's own death cannot be erased.

Sometimes it is best to lean into the sadness, to encourage the tears to come if they will, to share the sadness with our most trusted friends. But we need to guard against causing any sense of guilt. Our friend knows that we who love them are sad to see them suffer. They know we are torn—wanting a miracle and wanting them to be at rest.

Their sadness is deep—soul-piercing. You can see it in their eyes, though they don't talk about it much. Medical experts say that any change in our lives can result in physical and psychological damage. But even this does not fully explain how much it hurts.

Pause and rest awhile in the Lord's presence.

Gracious God, assure my friend that you will take care of us who survive, surrounding us with love and strength. We know that you won't erase our sadness in those weeks and months after our friend is gone, but that you will be there with us. I ask this humbly in the name of my friend _____ through Jesus Christ, my Lord. Amen.

Reflection

Quiet

Closing
Prayer

We Can and Must Trust in the Lord

Scripture | *Look how the wild flowers grow: they do not work or make clothes for themselves. But I tell you that not even King Solomon with all his wealth had clothes as beautiful as one of these flowers. It is God who clothes the wild grass....*

(Matthew 6:28-30)

Prayer | Lord, my friend trusts in you; they have grown up learning about trust, and now this challenge has tested their trust. You gave them trust as a birth-day gift, that is, a gift at birth. They have had their doubts like the rest of us, but meeting what life has brought has taught them that they cannot control every situation. Lord, help my friend to place their trust in you NOW.

Psalm | "The Destiny of the...Good"
Give yourself to the LORD;
    trust in him, and he will help you;
he will make your righteousness
    shine like the noonday sun.

(from Psalm 37)

Reflection | Learning to trust in another person is usually a long process. We meet someone; we become friends; we get to know them well. Then we are faced with a challenge, and we need help. At that point, we discover if our trust was well grounded. We ask of our friend, and they respond. The fact that we ask indicates our trust in them. The way they respond tells us whether our trust is justified.

Sometimes our trust in the Lord is challenged; we are faced with hardships we and our human support system cannot surmount. We ask the Lord for help, and the situation is not erased. We need to recall the times when we did place our trust in the Lord, when human intervention couldn't solve our problems. Perhaps reluctantly, we said to the Lord, "I give up. Take over, Lord." We surrendered our needs and problems to the Lord—without stopping our human efforts—and a solution was found. Remember, sometimes we do not gain what we originally asked for, but our attitude changes so that the answer makes sense.

Pause and rest awhile in the Lord's presence.

Quiet

Gracious God, never allow my friend to doubt that you are here to help them. The prospect of dying is not a matter we can solve alone; only you truly have all the answers. Reward my friend's trust in you. Whatever happens—sudden death or prolonged suffering—remind them of that birth-day gift. I ask this humbly in the name of my friend _____ through Jesus Christ, my Lord. Amen.

Closing Prayer

God Is Within Us

Scripture | *And the secret is that Christ is in you, which means that you will share in the glory of God. So we preach Christ to everyone.*
(Colossians 1:27-28)

Prayer | Lord, my friend feels so alone. Remind them that you are present within them. You have made a home in their heart, and this has made it possible for them to be open to the needs of others. Assure them that you are aware of their needs. Help them to feel your presence each moment.

Psalm | "The Goodness of God"
How precious, O God, is your constant love!
  We find protection under the
    shadow of your wings.
We feast on the abundant food you provide;
  you let us drink from the river of your goodness.
You are the source of all life,
  and because of your light we see the light.
(from Psalm 36)

Reflection | The words of a song called "From a Distance" describe how, from afar, the earth looks perfect and beautiful. There are no wars or hunger, the rivers are clean, and all the people live in harmony. The lyrics go on to say that we have to look closely to see that this is not a perfect world—that people who look similar to one another may be waging war, that some folks are wandering in the streets at night, homeless and starving.

I like that song, except for the last verse, which says that God looks on from a distance. No, our Lord is within each of us.

No matter how isolated and alone we may feel, we are never alone. Saint Paul calls this a secret, but everyone who truly believes knows that the presence of Christ in us makes us more than we appear to be; it gives us power. We can be open to our own needs and the needs of others; we can sense when a neighbor needs a word of encouragement; we can wipe away the tears of a frightened or fearful child. We have the strength, together with the help of the Lord within us, to meet whatever life sends us.

Pause and rest awhile in the Lord's presence.

Quiet

Gracious God, keep up my friend's strength a little longer. Having the Lord within them has made it possible for them to deal with whatever challenges they have had to deal with. No matter whatever else they have to suffer, grant them the peace of your presence within ALWAYS AND FOREVER. I ask this humbly in the name of my friend _____ through Jesus Christ, my Lord. Amen.

Closing Prayer

God Keeps Us Safe

Scripture *May the Lord himself, who is our source of peace, give you peace at all times and in every way.*

(2 Thessalonians 3:16)

Prayer | Lord, keep my friend safe. You have always been with them and within them. As a loving parent holds a frightened child, hold them close to your warm heart. Assure them that no matter what, they are safe in your loving care.

Psalm | "God Is With Us"
God is our shelter and strength,
   always ready to help in times of trouble.
So we will not be afraid,
      even if the earth is shaken
   and mountains fall into the ocean depths.

(from Psalm 46)

Reflection | As children, we had an essential need to feel safe. If we were fortunate, we found a sense of safety in our homes, in our family circle, in our school. We only feared what we did not know or understand—the dark, loud noises, family discord, violence, death.

As adults, most of us are no longer afraid of the dark. But there are times and situations in which we do not feel safe. When we are ill—really ill—we may not feel safe. This is because we all fear the unknown. We all like to feel in control of our lives and of our bodies, but sometimes we cannot be. The trouble is that when as adults we are ill or in danger, we become like lost children. We cannot find the Lord who is protecting us. We fear that we are alone and need to be reminded that the Lord is always there, to keep us safe.

Pause awhile and rest in the Lord's presence.

Quiet

Gracious God, remind my friend that you never leave them and that you will always protect them. Wrap them in your loving care and keep them safe. I ask this humbly in the name of my friend _____ through Jesus Christ, my Lord. Amen.

Closing Prayer

We Are Precious in the Sight of God

Scripture

Don't you know that your body is the temple of the Holy Spirit, who lives in you and who was given to you by God?
(1 Corinthians 6:19)

Prayer

Lord, remind my friend that they are a temple, despite the fact that their body is frail and invaded by illness. They need to know that they are even more precious to you now. Help them to feel special—it will mean so much to them.

Psalm

"In Praise of the Temple"
LORD, do not forget David
   and all the hardships he endured.
Remember, LORD, what he promised,
   the vow he made to you, the Mighty God of Jacob:
"I will not go home or go to bed;
   I will not rest or sleep,
   until I provide a place for the LORD,
   a home for the Mighty God of Jacob."

(from Psalm 132)

Reflection

A temple is a sacred place, a holy place—shining, meticulously pure, full of precious things—a fitting place for the Lord to dwell—a fitting place for us to meet the Lord in communion/prayer/worship.

The Spirit fills the heart that yearns to be filled with love, with grace, with all its gifts. The Spirit dwells in all of us, but some of us are aware, while others don't even realize it.

By welcoming the Spirit into the temple that we are, we gain strength and energy, the ability to share the Good News—not necessarily with words—but through what we are and how we deal with difficulties such as illness and dying.

Pause and rest awhile in the Lord's presence.

Quiet

Gracious God, remind my friend that they are an even more fitting vessel for you—because they have been, as they say, "tried by fire." Their suffering has made them somehow more beautiful and majestic—because you, Lord, go where you are welcome. Though my friend may not understand why there is so much pain, they turn to you for answers. Bless them, Lord. I ask this humbly in the name of my friend _____ through Jesus Christ, my Lord. Amen.

Closing Prayer

God Shows Us the Way

Scripture | *Let your hope keep you joyful, be patient in your troubles, and pray at all times.*

(Romans 12:12)

Prayer | Lord, be with my friend who is so tired. Remind them of those words by which they have lived their life. Grant them moments of peace and joy as they place their trust in you to take care of them; strengthen them with patience in these troubled times; they know that you lovingly listen to the constant simple prayer, "Lord, help me!" cherishing every word.

Psalm | "A Prayer of Thanksgiving"
When I am surrounded by troubles,
  you keep me safe.
You oppose my angry enemies
  and save me by your power.
You will do everything you have promised;
  LORD, your love is eternal.
  Complete the work that you have begun.

(from Psalm 138)

Reflection | Some people are openly spiritual people. Something about them sets them apart from the rest of us. They have learned to trust that the Lord will give them and all their loved ones whatever they need. They pray with faith, realizing that the Lord hears every prayer. They are open to whatever answer comes. They have gone through joy and pain, and they have survived.

Many of us when faced with challenges—illness or impending death—need a reminder that we are not being punished by

28

the illness that is slowly pulling the life out of us. The answer to that great mystery of life—why some good people suffer intensely and some prideful, selfish people seem to prosper—eludes us. When some trivial problem arises, we whine and complain. We don't know why life is like that.

Pause and rest awhile in the Lord's presence.

Quiet

Gracious God, reassure my friend that their life speaks for itself. There is no cause for concern if now that the end draws near, they do not feel joy, are tired of the pain, and cannot find the strength to pray. Their dying is a prayer. They are in labor to be reborn. Whether or not their life has been hopeful, prayerful, and joyful up to this point, Lord, be there to infuse these gifts now. I ask this humbly in the name of my friend _____ through Jesus Christ, my Lord. Amen.

Closing Prayer

God Has Made Us Rich in Spirit

Scripture

For in union with Christ you have become rich in all things, including all speech and all knowledge. The message about Christ has become so firmly established in you that you have not failed to receive a single blessing....

(1 Corinthians 1:5-7)

Prayer

Lord, stay close by my friend. Help them to know—to really be convinced—of the richness you have shared with them. Convince them that you will continue to shower them with your blessings.

Psalm

"Thanksgiving to God for His Justice"
I will praise you, LORD, with all my heart;
I will tell of all the wonderful
   things you have done.
I will sing with joy because of you.
  I will sing praise to you, Almighty God.

(from Psalm 9)

Reflection

We can be rich, even if we have few material possessions. We may have been raised in a family where we never lacked the necessities of life or even some of the luxuries. Or we may have come from humble roots, with a father who worked long hours and a mother who worked to make a spotless house and a warm and loving home.

No matter. We are rich in God's eyes. Preoccupied as we are with the terrible loss of a dear friend, we can hold on to the precious gift of their love. We can still recall with joy the times we spent together. We can remember special times, secrets we shared, songs we sang together. We can also be grateful for the special times we continue to share. We are privileged to be allowed to share our friend's last days on this earth.

Pause and rest awhile in the Lord's presence.

Gracious God, comfort my friend with the knowledge that they are rich—in faith, hope, and love. These are their treasures. Bless my friend and help them to continue to use their richness of spirit to bring strength and peace to the rest of us, who feel quite helpless now. I ask this humbly in the name of my friend _____ through Jesus Christ, my Lord. Amen.

Quiet

Closing
Prayer

God Gives Us Inner Strength

Scripture | *I ask God from the wealth of his glory to give you power through his Spirit to be strong in your inner selves, and I pray that Christ will make his home in your hearts through faith.*

(Ephesians 3:16-17)

Prayer | Lord, help my friend to be strong in their inner self. In the core of their inner being, with your grace, light that spark that has been quietly glowing through the years. Inflame my friend with strength.

Psalm | "A Prayer for Inner Strength"
But I will sing about your strength;
  every morning I will sing aloud
    of your constant love.
You have been a refuge for me,
  a shelter in my time of trouble.
I will praise you, my defender.
  My refuge is God,
    the God who loves me.

(from Psalm 59)

Reflection | Jesus once said, "I have come to light a fire on this earth." He came to light a fire in each one of us who believes. That fire never goes out unless we choose to put it out. And when we need more power than usual—when we are in great peril or when we are suffering intensely—that inner strength is there, waiting to be tapped.

When people are dying, they need to be inflamed with the fire of the Lord. Their bodies are weak, but their spirits are will-

32

ing and yearning to be alive—forever. The trouble is that dying may be accompanied by exhaustion; those who are preparing to leave this earthly life may be so tired that it is hard to think. And this is understandable—we must fall asleep before we can reawaken in heaven, the fullness of the kingdom.

Pause and rest awhile in the Lord's presence.

Quiet

Gracious God, make my friend warm with your loving spirit, like a blazing fire of light, to give them strength. Allow their love to shine through like a flaming sunset. Allow their union with you to shine through like lightning in the summer sky. Lord, keep them warm as they have brought warmth to those of us who love them. I ask this humbly in the name of my friend _____ through Jesus Christ, my Lord. Amen.

Closing Prayer

God Grants Us Serenity

Scripture | *Your life in Christ makes you strong, and his love comforts you. You have fellowship with the Spirit, and you have kindness and compassion for one another.*

(Philippians 2:1)

Prayer | Lord, help my friend to continue to be serene. Just as their serenity has enabled them to be a source of peace and calm for others in times of difficulty, comfort them now and help them to pray, "God, grant me the serenity to accept the things I cannot change, the courage to change the things I can, and the wisdom to know the difference."

Psalm | "A Prayer of Confidence"
And so I am thankful and glad,
   and I feel completely secure,
because you protect me from the
     power of death.
I have served you faithfully,
   and you will not abandon me
   to the world of the dead.

You will show me the path that leads to life;
   your presence fills me with joy
   and brings me pleasure forever.

(from Psalm 16)

Reflection | Anyone who can remain serene in times of crisis is to be admired. But we must keep in mind that serenity is not something innate. We develop serenity; we learn serenity—not in school but through living out our lives.

Serenity. Repeat that word several times. The word itself is lyrical, musical. Some people use this word as a technique for reinforcing their strength in times of difficulty. They picture a scene that evokes serenity and dwell on it, entering into it for a few moments. Then they go on with their day, actually feeling more serene. When a person is seriously ill, when a person is dying, they are often increasingly limited. If they can appreciate their small accomplishments, they will be able to maintain serenity. Even something that may seem insignificant, like a shadow of a smile, bespeaks serenity.

Pause and rest awhile in the Lord's presence.

Quiet

Gracious God, grant my friend true serenity. They may cry or become frustrated. That is perfectly acceptable; it is healthy. But allow them to return to your loving arms and rest there. I humbly ask this in the name of my friend _____ through Jesus Christ, my Lord. Amen.

Closing
Prayer

God Desires Our Love

"And now I give you a new commandment: love one another. As I have loved you, so you must love one another...then everyone will know that you are my disciples."

(John 13:34-35)

Prayer

Lord, as you know, my friend is a down-to-earth, real person, but their life has told of their love for you; it is a psalm, a sacred song. Remind them that soon you will meet in a special way; help them to concentrate on that holy meeting and allow the rest of their thoughts to drift away from the painful aspects of their death to the glory that will follow.

Psalm

"A Song of Victory"
How I love you, LORD!
   You are my defender.

The LORD is my protector;
   he is my strong fortress.
My God is my protection,
   and with him I am safe.

(from Psalm 18)

Reflection

Love—what is it? People have trouble defining love because its meaning is different for each of us. The two great commandments that Jesus gave us concerned love: to love the Lord God with our whole being and to love one another for the love of God.

One of life's greatest paradoxes is that there are many loving people, but the depth of their love is not related to the amount of suffering in their lives. Once again, we must remember that suffering is not a punishment from God; it is not a sign of the withdrawal of God's love from us. God's love is the source of our strength during our times of greatest difficulty.

Pause and rest awhile in the Lord's presence.

Quiet

Gracious God, remind my friend that you know how they love you. It is precisely that love that will help them not simply to endure but to master this process of dying. Remind them that you have not withdrawn your love—and they know it. Give them a strong dose of your protective love NOW, when they really need it. I ask this humbly in the name of my friend _____ through Jesus Christ, my Lord. Amen.

Closing Prayer

God Is Not Unfair

Scripture | *God is not unfair. He will not forget the work you did or the love you showed for him in the help you gave and are still giving to your fellow Christians.*

(Hebrews 6:10)

Prayer | Lord, remind my friend that you are not unfair. They not only spent their life as a loving, faithful person, but even in their illness they are helping others with their strong spirit, quiet acceptance, and gentle preparation for what is to come. You remember all the good they have done; now you see them doing good each moment.

Psalm | "A Prayer for Justice"
But you do see; you take notice
    of trouble and suffering,
  and are always ready to help.
The helpless man commits himself to you;
    you have always helped the needy.

(from Psalm 10)

Reflection | Most of us work in a circle that is not very large: family, neighbors, church friends, perhaps coworkers. We do our best in our corner of the world to meet the needs of those around us. And when one of these people is ill and dying, it seems unfair.

These days my friend is dealing with this seeming unfairness. They may be very angry at the injustice of dying, though we know that we will all die. I don't know whether they express their anger verbally or whether they are angry at the doctors or the hospitals or at life in general. Even people who hardly

38

ever express anger—when faced with the prospect of untimely death—get angry! Life is not always fair, but the Lord is.

Pause and rest awhile in the Lord's presence.

Quiet

Gracious God, remind my friend once again that you are not oblivious to what they are going through. This illness is not from you; it is not a test; it is not a punishment; it is not an opportunity for salvation; it is not their fault. In the middle of the night, when they can't sleep because of the pain or the fear, remind them that you remember the good they have done—not because the more we do, the more you love us, but because there is much more good for them to do even after they leave this earth. I ask this humbly in the name of my friend _____ through Jesus Christ, my Lord. Amen.

Closing
Prayer

God Empowers Us to Make Decisions

Scripture | *For the Spirit that God has given us does not make us timid; instead, his Spirit fills us with power, love, and self-control.*

(2 Timothy 1:7)

Prayer | Lord, help my friend during these final days as they and their family are called upon to make major decisions, perhaps concerning whether to continue or discontinue treatment. There may be family matters to be acted upon, legal affairs to be completed, even funeral preferences to be discussed. Help my friend have the power to stay in control of their life.

Psalm | "A Prayer of Confidence"
You, LORD, are all I have,
   and you give me all I need;
   my future is in your hands.
How wonderful are your gifts to me;
   how good they are!

. . . .

I am always aware of the LORD's presence;
   he is near, and nothing can shake me.

(from Psalm 16)

Reflection | Sometimes it's only in looking back that we recognize how strong we have been. The story of the mother who works up enough adrenaline to lift a car in order to free her child who is trapped beneath its wheels is well known. We surprise ourselves by the strength we can muster in times of need.

People who know they are dying are usually most at peace when they feel they have some control over what is happening to them. If they are alert and know and understand what their status is, they should have the right to make decisions. People who have made a habit of relying on the Lord for guidance are already empowered.

Pause awhile and rest in the Lord's presence.

Gracious God, continue to fill my friend with the power that comes from you. They have prayed for your guidance. They have consulted with physicians and family. They have searched their own soul, opening themselves, as always, to your influence. Be with them, whatever is decided. I ask this humbly in the name of my friend _____ through Jesus Christ, my Lord. Amen.

Quiet

Closing
Prayer

God Grants Us Endurance

Scripture | *We also boast of our troubles, because we know that trouble produces endurance, endurance brings God's approval, and his approval creates hope.*

(Romans 5:3-4)

Prayer | Lord, hold my friend close to your heart. Carry them in your arms; they have endured much. If they could have willed their healing, they would have found health a long time ago; they have never given up trying. Lord, continue to grant them the strength to endure, until you call them home.

Psalm | "A Prayer for Help in Time of Trouble"
I am worn out, O LORD; have pity on me!
  Give me strength; I am completely exhausted
  and my whole being is deeply troubled.
How long, O LORD, will you wait to help me?

(from Psalm 6)

Reflection | Paul, in his letter to the Romans, told his followers about his troubles because they were an education in endurance for him. He suffered in many ways, though he had indeed been called by God in a rather dramatic way to stop persecuting Christians, to gain their trust somehow, then to preach the Good News to them. When he "boasted" of his pain, he was not being conceited. On the contrary, he was humbled by the knowledge that God called him to endure pain, humiliation, imprisonment, as a way of showing others that those whom God has chosen may be asked to endure much.

My friend has surely endured—pain, loss, weakness, helplessness. They are tired of the pain. What more do you expect of them? They have done it all. We need to learn from my friend that when our path is dark and we see no hope, we could be mistaken. We may be very close to turning the corner to the entrance to the light. Lord, help us and help them to not give up.

Pause and rest awhile in the Lord's presence.

Gracious God, my friend has surely proved their endurance—beyond all expectations. They live what they know are their final days as fully as possible, cherishing each moment. At the same time, they are slowly detaching themselves from earthly concerns. When will you say, "Enough is enough"? I know the answer: when the time is right. My friend has been on your mind for all time. Keep them going until you escort them regally into the fullness of the kingdom. I ask this humbly in the name of my friend _____ through Jesus Christ, my Lord. Amen.

Quiet

Closing
Prayer

God Wants Us to Be Gentle

Scripture | *Show a gentle attitude toward everyone. The Lord is coming soon. Don't worry about anything, but in your prayers ask God for what you need, always asking him with a thankful heart. And God's peace, which is far beyond human understanding, will keep your hearts and minds safe in union with Christ Jesus.*
(Philippians 4:5-7)

Prayer | Lord, help my friend to be gentle with their own self. Remind them that you love them and will continue to see to their needs as you always have. Also, Lord—model of gentleness—be gentle with them. They are very fragile now, tired and a bit frightened. Take their hand now and assure them that you will not let go until they are safely on the other side.

Psalm | "The Lord Our Shepherd"
The LORD is my shepherd;
  I have everything I need.
He lets me rest in fields of green grass
  and leads me to quiet pools of fresh water.
He gives me new strength.
He guides me in the right paths,
  as he has promised.
Even if I go through the deepest darkness,
  I will not be afraid, LORD,
  for you are with me.
Your shepherd's rod and staff protect me.
(from Psalm 23)

Reflection | Some of us are more gentle by nature than others, but there are ways each of us can express the gentleness that Jesus

44

taught. No matter how tough we appear on the outside, we can find a gentle spot in our heart and allow that seed to grow until it envelops us.

Now, as we prepare for the death of our friend, we may express our gentleness in various ways:

- by comforting our children, who are sad and confused that someone they love is about to leave them behind;
- by mixing our own tears with those of someone else who loves our friend;
- by calming friends who have come to say their good-byes but who are distraught and perhaps apologetic about not having spent more time when the dying person was well;
- by refusing to be drawn into senseless arguments, which are usually manifestations of everyone's helplessness;
- by putting aside any bitterness or anger toward someone who has caused us pain, who now returns to pay their respects.

Pause and rest awhile in the Lord's presence.

Quiet

Gracious God, we minimize the greatness of our gifts. Help my friend to know, somehow, how much their gentleness, however well hidden, has affected those around them. Those who love them so much know that they are God's gift to us. Lord, bless my friend for their gentleness, whose effects will remain long after they have died. I ask this humbly in the name of my friend _____ through Jesus Christ, my Lord. Amen.

Closing
Prayer

God Is as Eager for Reunion as We Are

Scripture | *Be patient, then, my brothers [and sisters], until the Lord comes. See how patient a farmer is as he waits for his land to produce precious crops. He waits patiently for the autumn and spring rains. You also must be patient. Keep your hopes high, for the day of the Lord's coming is near.*

(James 5:7-8)

Prayer | Lord, my friend is waiting for you to come for them and bring them into the fullness of the kingdom. They wait through this long night—through the pain, the sadness, the resignation, the freeing of their soul through acceptance. Lord, wait with them.

Psalm | "A Prayer for Help"
I wait eagerly for the LORD's help,
   and in his word I trust.
I wait for the Lord
   more eagerly than watchmen wait
      for the dawn—
   than watchmen wait for the dawn.

(from Psalm 130)

Reflection | There was a violent storm last night. Thunder crashed around us. Lightning lit up the sky. Sharp winds blew angrily. Tornadoes were sighted in the area. Trees were uprooted, and large branches are strewn everywhere today. The power failed in some towns, including ours, so we had no lights in the house and no streetlights.

46

How long the night seems when there is no light! Our few candles could not penetrate the darkness. I was afraid. I had a sense of lurking danger, a feeling of helplessness against the storm. Many years ago, when Jesus was on this earth, watchmen stood by the city gates to protect the inhabitants from invasion by strangers. These sentinels had to stay awake and alert through the blackest of nights, awaiting the dawn. We need to remember that no matter how dark our life may seem, dawn will come.

Pause and rest awhile in the Lord's presence.

Quiet

Gracious God, help my friend not to fear the darkness. Grant me the strength to keep prayerful vigil over my friend. Grant them your loving care and the blessing of a good night's sleep, the sleep of a child, deep and replenishing. Tell my friend once again that when they go to sleep for the last time, they will awaken to the dawn of your eternal kingdom. I ask this humbly in the name of my friend _____ through Jesus Christ, my Lord. Amen.

Closing
Prayer

We Will Be Reborn When We Die

Scripture

When a woman is about to give birth, she is sad because her hour of suffering has come; but when the baby is born, she forgets her suffering, because she is happy that a baby has been born into the world. That is how it is with you: now you are sad, but I will see you again, and your hearts will be filled with gladness, the kind of gladness that no one can take away from you.

(John 16:21-22)

Prayer

Lord, fill my friend with the hope that as they close their eyes to this earthly life, they will be reborn in heaven. My friend is fearful; this is understandable, for giving birth always causes pain. Remind my friend that whatever they suffer as they are dying will be replaced by the joy of their rebirth.

Psalm

"A Prayer of Praise"
It was you who brought me safely through birth,
   and when I was a baby, you kept me safe.
I have relied on you since the day I was born,
   and you have always been my God.

(from Psalm 22)

Birth involves coming forth from the safety of the mother's womb, perhaps with great struggle for many hours, into bright lights, noise, and excitement. A child is born! Alleluia! The Lord brought my friend safely through this first birth, and now it seems that the Lord is preparing them for a birth of a different sort. How can we prepare to meet the Lord if we have not met him while on this earth? If your lives have not been a day-by-day preparation for the final transition—what will happen? We just don't know. Some people leave this world violently in a car crash, some suddenly after a heart attack or stroke. Some never feel a thing. Others, like my friend, are ill, and their illness allows them some time to prepare for the wonderful rebirth.

Pause and rest awhile in the Lord's presence.

Gracious God, help my friend as they await the "labor pains"— the signs that you are calling them to you. Banish their fears. I know you have been at work in them; they seem prepared. Stay with them, Lord. I ask this humbly in the name of my friend _____ through Jesus Christ, my Lord. Amen.

Reflection

Quiet

Closing Prayer

God Helps Us Prepare to Say Our Good-Byes

Scripture | *Jesus answered, "Whoever drinks this [well] water will get thirsty again, but whoever drinks the water that I will give him will never be thirsty again. The water that I will give him will become in him a spring which will provide him with life-giving water and give him eternal life."*

(John 4:13-14)

Prayer | Lord, my friend is parched and unable to quench the thirst. They thirst for you, not just to glimpse you for an instant but to remain in your presence always. Be with them as they await the appointed hour.

Psalm | "A Prayer of Hope"
As a deer longs for a stream of cool water,
   so I long for you, O God.
I thirst for you, the living God.
   When can I go and worship in your presence?

(from Psalm 42)

Reflection | On a hot summer day, when we are parched from the heat, nothing quenches our thirst like pure, cold water. If we cannot drink that water, we become dehydrated and may even faint. The image of a deer searching for a stream of cool water is lovely. Animals know instinctively where to look for the fulfillment of their needs.

We human beings need the Lord to fill our most important needs. When people die slowly, they are getting ready for the journey. In a sense, they are packing, collecting their memories, causing their loved ones to come together. We all need to know that our loved ones will be able to go on without us, that they are willing, albeit reluctantly, to say their good-byes to us, and that they will be able to take care of themselves.

Pause and rest awhile in the Lord's presence.

Quiet

Gracious God, help my friend with the hardest part of dying—saying good-bye to the rest of us, if not in words, then in loving gestures or silent communication. Medical experts say that possibly even those in a coma hear what is being said in their presence. Therefore, it is essential that we surround our dying friend with a sense of peace. When the time comes, they will leave the rest of us behind, but they will be waiting for us to join them. Help them and us to be ready. I ask this humbly in the name of my friend _____ through Jesus Christ, my Lord. Amen.

Closing
Prayer

God Hears and Answers Our Prayers for the Dying

Scripture

And so I [Jesus] say to you: Ask, and you will receive; seek, and you will find; knock, and the door will be opened to you. For everyone who asks will receive, and he who seeks will find, and the door will be opened to anyone who knocks.

(Luke 11:9-10)

Prayer

Lord, my friend has always prayed for others in need. Listen to my friend now as they pray for themselves. Now, when it appears that the end is really near, my friend is caught between two natural inclinations: to pray for a miracle or to pray to die soon and thus spare themselves and others further pain. Reassure them once again that you will give them whatever they need and will take care of them whatever the outcome.

Psalm

"Evening Prayer for Help"
Answer me when I pray,
   O God, my defender!
When I was in trouble, you helped me.
   Be kind to me now and hear my prayer.

(from Psalm 4)

Reflection

Close friends often say to one another, "You are in my thoughts and prayers." We think of and pray for those whom we love. When someone is seriously ill and in danger of dying, some of us try to figure out what would be best for our friend.

The trouble with doing this is that we don't stop to think that only God knows what is best. I think that if we really meant it when we say, "Your will be done," we would not have this dilemma.

Let's ask the Lord to give our friend the true answer to their prayers—and the strength to accept the Lord's answer, whatever it is.

Pause and rest awhile in the Lord's presence.

Quiet

Gracious God, make your will known; answer my friend's prayers and join my prayers to theirs. You know us and you love us. In the end, if we allow you to work in and through us, everything will come out all right. Help our trust in your judgment, Lord, to remain strong. And if it is your will that my friend die now, then be there to wipe away the tears of those of us who love them; help us to deal with our great loss. I ask this in the name of my friend _____ through Jesus Christ, my Lord. Amen.

Closing Prayer

God Keeps Us Going

Scripture | *We are often troubled, but not crushed; sometimes in doubt, but never in despair; there are many enemies, but we are never without a friend; and though badly hurt at times, we are not destroyed. At all times we carry in our mortal bodies the death of Jesus, so that his life may also be seen in our bodies.*

(2 Corinthians 4:8-10)

Prayer | Lord, reassure my friend, who believes they have failed in many areas. Remind them that our feelings of failure, of despair, of isolation, of being destroyed, are understandable. But you can lift my friend onto your shoulders and raise them above the dark pit into which they fear they will fall.

Psalm | "A Prayer for Help"
How much longer will you forget me, LORD?
  Forever?
How much longer will you hide yourself from me?
How long must I endure trouble?
  How long will sorrow fill
    my heart day and night?
How long will my enemies triumph over me?

(from Psalm 13)

Reflection | My friend has told me that the words of this Psalm don't make sense to them. They are indeed in trouble, and they do feel crushed. Yes, they are alive, but just barely. They feel as if they have been hit by a series of tractor-trailer trucks. Yes, it does seem as if there is an enemy trying to kill them, and even their best friend cannot bring consolation. They have had their doubts and have felt desperate, willing to do almost anything to end the suffering. My friend has been badly hurt, and the life is slowly being pulled out of their body.

We need to remind ourselves that nothing can take away our eternal life. Once created, we will live forever. We may be physically and psychologically crushed, but nothing—no illness, no power on earth—can crush our immortal soul. We may despair at finding a solution to our earthly problems, but we can trust in the Lord to keep us in his loving care.

Pause and rest awhile in the Lord's presence.

Quiet

Gracious God, renew my friend's unshakable faith in you. Promise them that you will stand by them and never abandon them. Even at death, their life in Christ will continue. Grant to my friend, whom I love dearly, life everlasting. I seek this humbly in the name of my friend _____ through Jesus Christ, my Lord. Amen.

Closing Prayer

God Helps Us To Sing

Scripture *I will sing with my spirit, but I will sing also with my mind.*

(1 Corinthians 14:15)

Prayer | Lord, give my friend pleasure in singing to you with their heart and soul, not with lyric and melody, but with bits and pieces of thoughts and memories that come to them during the day—pieces of the mosaic of their life. Fill their mind with pleasant memories and thoughts; grant them insight about the present days; flood them with hope for the future of those dear to them.

Psalm | "A Prayer of Thanksgiving"
You have changed my sadness
    into a joyful dance;
  you have taken away my sorrow
    and surrounded me with joy.
So I will not be silent;
  I will sing praise to you.
LORD, you are my God;
I will give you thanks forever.

(from Psalm 30)

Reflection | We sing for many reasons: in times of celebration, such as holidays or Sunday worship, when we are full of sadness and cannot speak, as at a funeral. We sing because lyric and melody together can bring us peace, or perhaps we love poetry set to music. Sometimes we sing simply because a particular song on the radio moves us in some way.

We don't need to be poets or musicians to sing with our spirit. We simply need to be "in tune" with God's will. And we can know God's will by being ourselves, by asking every day that the Lord lead us where he may. We can sing also with our mind, reflecting and meditating upon what our life means. We need to take time to look at the broader picture of our life, trying to pull it all together and make sense of it. Dying people do this easily, but it can be a difficult exercise for those of us still at midcourse.

Pause and rest awhile in the Lord's presence.

Quiet

Gracious God, help my friend as they try, in their final days, to put together the mosaic of their life. They are deeply reflective now, open to the hymns you sing to them. Help them find peace by singing to you with spirit and mind. I ask this humbly in the name of my friend _____ through Jesus Christ, my Lord. Amen.

Closing Prayer

God Will Take Away All Our Pain

Scripture

I consider that what we suffer at this present time cannot be compared at all with the glory that is going to be revealed to us.

(Romans 8:18)

Prayer

Lord, stay close to my friend in their suffering. They are in great pain and recently talked about being "so tired." They told me, "You get to the point where you wonder how much longer this can go on." Lord, my friend needs to be wrapped in the protective warm blanket of your love—*now*. Please hurry.

Psalm

"A Cry for Help"
Save me, O God!
　The water is up to my neck;
I am sinking in deep mud,
　and there is no solid ground;
I am out in deep water,
　and the waves are about to drown me.
I am worn out from calling for help,
　and my throat is aching.
I have strained my eyes,
　looking for your help.

(from Psalm 69)

Reflection

It is so hard to stand by and watch someone we love suffer. We know they do not deserve to suffer like this. We need to remember that no pain, no matter how excruciating, goes on forever. But this is small comfort as we watch our friend try to be brave but lose the ability to contain their cries of pain. We may say, "Squeeze my hand," and the direction of our friend's energy is shifted away from the center of pain and toward the outstretched hand. The pain of their squeezing hard our own hand is only a mild reflection of the pain they are feeling.

Pause and rest awhile in the Lord's presence.

Quiet

Gracious God, reach out your hand to my friend and encourage them to squeeze hard. When the crushing pain comes, over and over, direct their energy in your direction. Remind them that you are strong enough to bear that pain, that you will remain there all the way, that you *will not* let go. I ask this humbly in the name of my friend _____ through Jesus Christ, my Lord. Amen.

Closing
Prayer

God Will Escort Us Into Heaven

Scripture *"Do not be worried and upset," Jesus told them. "Believe in God and believe also in me. There are many rooms in my Father's house, and I am going to prepare a place for you....I will come back and take you to myself, so that you will be where I am."*

(John 14:1-3)

Prayer Lord, remind my friend, who has begun to withdraw from us, that when the time comes, you will escort them into the place of light where they *live* eternally in your presence, in the presence of their loved ones who have gone before them, and with all the faithful.

Psalm "A Hymn of Praise"
The LORD is good;
  his love is eternal
  and his faithfulness lasts forever.

(from Psalm 100)

Reflection We really do not know what happens at death. We have been taught to believe that the kingdom of God is now and forever. In the now, there are pains and struggles, joys and sorrows; there is *waiting*. At death, we make the transition to the fullness of the kingdom, which we have been told is heaven.

People who have been revived after so-called "near-death" experiences tell us that they feel differently about life. They no longer fear dying. Somehow, they have returned to the *now* after a brief glimpse of the *light.* For the rest of their lives on this earth, they long to return to the hereafter. Some say they become more attuned to God's presence in their lives as a result of their experience. They become God-centered people in the world of the now. We can become God-centered, too, without a near-death experience, but we need to set our priorities now, not when death confronts us.

Pause and rest awhile in the Lord's presence.

Quiet

Gracious God, help my friend as they seem to be accepting the reality, the immediacy, of their death. Remind them that you have already prepared a place for them to go; everything is ready. Despite my friend's reluctance to leave the rest of us behind, Lord, bless them with the detachment to say farewell, even if they are in a coma. Grant them the strength to walk through the long tunnel into the bright Light, our God. I ask this humbly in the name of my friend _____ through Jesus Christ, my Lord. Amen.

Closing Prayer

God Calls Us Home

Scripture | *"Wake up, sleeper,*
and rise from death,
and Christ will shine on you."

(Ephesians 5:14)

Prayer | Lord, there is nothing left to say. Words do not come. Thoughts do not come. But you know what is in my heart.

Psalm | "A Prayer of Glory"
Wake up, my soul!
  Wake up, my harp and lyre!
  I will wake up the sun.
I will thank you, O Lord, among the nations.
  I will praise you among the peoples.

(from Psalm 57)

Reflection | My friend has died. I just heard, and, of course, the tears come—tears of sadness for the loss of my friend's physical presence in my life and tears of joy that at last they are at peace.

Now my friend has awakened; the sun and the moon are theirs; every grace and blessing are theirs. They fell asleep alive, and this day they have awakened in heaven.

The white light of God's glory shines upon them. There are no shadows, only light, because God's light fills heaven. Not only does my friend live in the presence of God now—the goal of an entire lifetime—they have rejoined those loves ones who went before them and whom they have longed to see again.

Pause and rest awhile in the Lord's presence.

Gracious God, wake up my friend! So many nights recently, they have lain in bed and wondered whether they would see the dawn. This day they have been filled with the light of your dawn. They have assumed a new perspective: they are now on the inside, by your side, surrounded by all the faithful who have gone before them. And this dawn will never end. All the sunrises and sunsets, all the beautiful experiences they had while on earth, are as darkness compared with your heavenly light, which is forever.

Bless my friend and keep them in your loving care until we meet again. Amen. Alleluia!

Quiet

Closing Prayer

Epilogue

I look to the mountains;
  where will my help come from?
My help will come from the LORD,
  who made heaven and earth.

He will not let you fall;
  your protector is always awake.

The protector of Israel
  never dozes or sleeps.

. . . .

The LORD will protect you from all danger;
  he will keep you safe.
He will protect you as you come and go
  now and forever.

(from Psalm 121)